ALL I NEED TO KNOW I LEARNED FROM MY CAT DEAD

Written by Jim Becker & Andy Mayer
Illustrated by Chuck Reasoner

A Perigee Book

Perigee Books
are published by
The Putnam Publishing Group
200 Madison Avenue
New York, NY 10016

Library of Congress Cataloging-in-Publication Data

Becker, Jim.
All I need to know I learned from my dead cat / written by Jim
Becker & Andy Mayer ; illustrated by Chuck Reasoner.
p. cm.
ISBN 0-399-51681-6 (alk. paper)
1. Cats—Caricatures and cartoons. 2. American wit and humor,
Pictorial. I. Mayer, Andrew, date. II. Reasoner, Charles.
III. Title.
NC1429.B3514A4 1991   91-3148 CIP
741.5′973—dc20

Printed in the United States of America

1 2 3 4 5 6 7 8 9 10

This book is printed on acid-free paper.

Be supportive.

Only use manufacturer's recommended replacement parts.

Don't play with loaded guns.

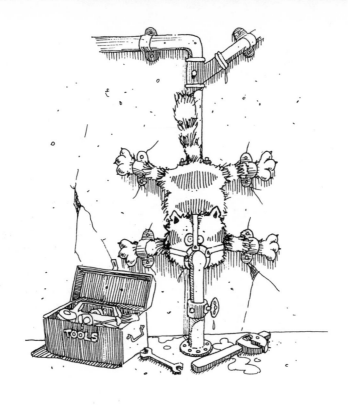

Only call the plumber as a last resort.

Keep your elbows off the table.

Don't move if you suspect spinal injuries.

Go with the flow.

Some people are just prone to accidents.

Learn to share.

Work hard.

Play hard.

Some people will do anything to get attention.

Kids will be kids.

If anything can go wrong, it will.

Life is full of mysteries.

Pets can be a great comfort in old age.

Always clean up after yourself.

Don't overextend yourself.

Recycle. Every little bit counts.

Monkey see, monkey do.

There's no such thing as a happy ending.

ELAPSED TIME:

9 DAYS

14 HOURS

51 MINUTES

07 SECONDS

**There's more to life than getting into the
Guinness Book of World Records.**

It's the little touches that make a house a home.

When your number's up, it's up.

If it says don't touch, it means don't touch.

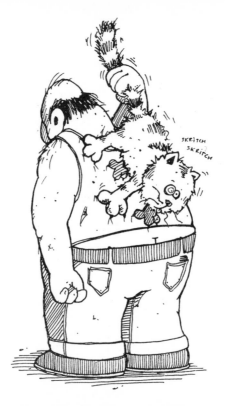

If it itches, scratch it.

There's nothing like the smell of Christmas.

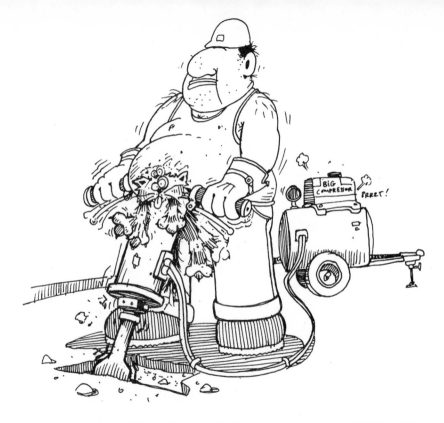

A little hard work never hurt anybody.

Who needs Toys "Я" Us?

If you don't succeed, try, try again.

Bar bets can get out of hand.

**Sometimes you can tell which way the train came
by just looking at the tracks.**

There's nothing like the feel of natural fibers.

A power tool doesn't always make the job go faster.

Who needs Sears?

Live for the moment.

Things always turn up where you least expect them.

A sucker is born every minute.

**Who says you can't be in two places
at the same time?**

Wake up and smell the coffee.

Any meat works in meatloaf.

Where there's smoke, there's something smoking.

Everyone's a joker.

Baseball...What a game!

Enjoy life, eat out more often.

Use your head.

Safety first.

Who says three can't play Ping-Pong?

Live life to its fullest.

Everyone loves 4th of July.

Relax...Enjoy life's simple pleasures.

Never go to sleep in the disposal.

Super glue really does glue just about anything.

If it doesn't move, and it's flat like a pancake, chances are it's dead.

Life's a bitch.

You've got to plow into your work headfirst.

Grin and bear it.

Nothing in life is easy.

Irregularity is a pain in the ass.

Cutting energy costs

Insulate.

is a piece of cake.

Burn alternative fuels.

When in Rome, do what a Roman does.

Sometimes you have to kiss ass.

You can never tell what's in the bottom of a trash compacter unless you put your head right down into it and take a look.

**Some methods of flea control
are more effective than others.**

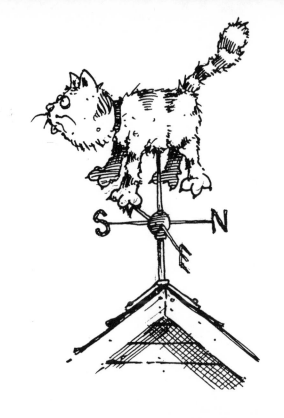

Everybody is good at something.

Keep a stiff upper lip.

There's no fighting gravity.

**Just because you're dead,
doesn't mean you can't have a good time!**

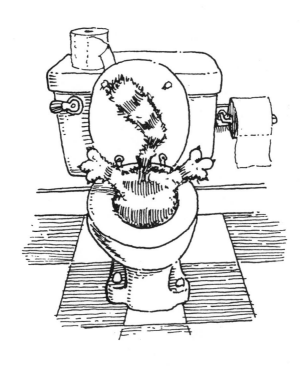

Wait at least one hour before swimming.

Go for the gusto!

Everyone loves frozen food.

**Sometimes you don't go to Heaven or Hell
you just kinda stick around.**

Circuit breakers don't always work.

A good friend is hard to find.

Life is a game of inches.

A good luck charm will only get you so many spares.

**What's the big deal about having nine lives
if you die every time?**